PRAYERS A DAY

7 7 7

7 7 7

7 7 7

7 7 7

"**Seven** times a day I praise you for your righteous laws."
(Psalm 119:164)

This is a little book to help people stop, pray and remember. It is designed for use in a busy day, or when, and if, people do not know how to pray, or even feel that they cannot. It is ecumenical, for all Christians. Some will be used to forms of liturgical prayer, others will not. For some, daily prayers will be longer and more formal, for others simpler and extemporary, free prayer. The form of these prayers is brief, simple and accessible (although even a short prayer can go deep when actually prayed!). Even so, such a basic structure can sometimes be too much and if a few things can resonate, be taken up and used, if only in a prayer of a simple action and a few words, may they bring blessing.

The first Christians developed various ways of daily prayer. They would have still used Jewish prayers, and their own, often free prayer (sometimes being 'charismatic'). A very early text (the

Didache, late first century?) advocates saying the Our Father three times a day. There were three sacrificial services in the Jerusalem Temple, and this might have been behind this exhortation. By the third century, seven times were being taught, following on from the Jewish tradition that could be found in the Old Testament, as quoted above. Seven was a sacred number for Judaism, after all. Did anyone actually pray seven times daily? Perhaps some did, but this could have been symbolic of taking sacred time out to pray. One Christian writer, Hippolytus, in the 3rd century AD, asked believers to offer prayers upon rising, the lighting of the morning lamp, bedtime and midnight. Three other times were added at the third hour, the sixth and the ninth hour. The recitation of the Old Testament Psalms (a word meaning 'praises' from Greek and Latin) became formalised by the monk, Benedict of Nursia, in the sixth century AD and the monks sought to recite all 150 Psalms (though later translations have 149, note[1]) in the course of their regular prayers. Recitation of the Psalms became normative for many Christian liturgies, as it can be today for some, though often outside monasteries or convents, this is three times per day.

The Old Testament Psalms are a collection of prayers that can be outpourings of prayer, poetry or songs. Some are short or very long. They cover praise, joy, fear, intercession, prophecy, hope, and some nasty elements, such as wishing death and disaster upon enemies. (Remember that these were written many years before Jesus when not as much had been revealed about God and some attitudes were different.) They became a very useful way of praying the various aspects of the ups and downs of life. Eastern monks also developed the idea of reciting the Jesus Prayer, 'Lord Jesus Christ, Son of God, have mercy on me'. This could be shortened to simply 'Jesus'. In the West, the rosary with its fifteen decades (sets of ten beads) provided a simpler, popular form of devotion rather than reciting 150 Psalms.

Seven times a day? We are not monks or nuns! Respecting that, and working for all Christians of all traditions, I present a simple formula for each of the set times. These are suggestions. Some may wish to extend these, others may only be able to stop, think and utter few words, maybe even a single word, if troubled or unsure of what to do. There is a creative section at the

---

[1] The translation used here, the New International Version, uses 149 Psalms. This translation is in common use among many Christians. Catholics and Eastern Orthodox would have versions with 150. It is all about splitting some into two, rather than being a single Psalm. There are no new or different texts.

end to encourage people to have symbols, objects or actions that can be used as a reminder of each time of prayer. Perhaps a string of beads, a bracelet, a small stone or pebbles in a bowl. Make a movement like holding up your hands, crossing yourself, kneeling or similar. I hope that you may be able to create seven simple objects, ideally. If not, one will suffice, like a small cross to hold, or one of those stones with FAITH or LOVE, for example, written on them. Placed in the pocket, with a touch, then one of these can stop and anchor, even if you pray only a few words or many. Some may use holy pictures, Icons, with pictures of Jesus and the Saints. Eastern Orthodox Christians often have an icon corner in their homes where they stand to pray. This may be too much for some people's spirituality. Whatever you find useful. The seven prayer times used here are: Dawn, Morning, Elevenses, Noon, Afternoon, Evening and Night. The book is very visual. We use more than words as human beings. An image can evoke feelings. Use them in your prayers, also. Above all, be you, find your feet. These are guidelines. You may only feel able to do one or two each day. That is up to you. May this little book help you to take time out, to stop, to give thanks and to wonder.

"Be still and know that I am God." (Psalm 46:10)

DAWN

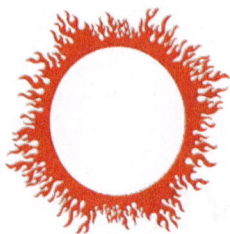

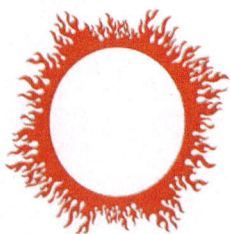

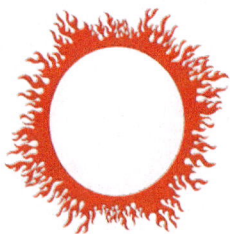

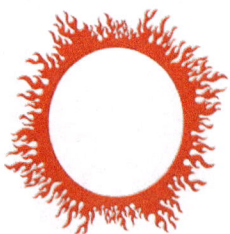

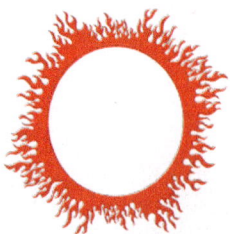

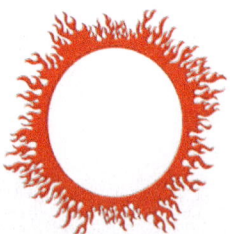

FOCUS

In the name of the Father, and the Son, and the Holy Spirit.

Let my soul rise to meet you as the day rises to meet the sun

Those who hope in the Lord will renew their strength.
They will soar on wings like eagles, they will run and not grow weary,
they will walk and not be faint. (Isaiah 40:30-31).

Be still. Breath slowly. Give thanks.

TOUCH

We are more than our minds and our feelings. We are bodies. Respond and pray with the body.

Light a candle?
Burn some incense?
Hold a prayer bead or stone?
Sprinkle some water over your face?
Stand or kneel?
Make the sign of the cross?
Hold out your open hands?

WELCOME

A prayer of introduction, welcome and praise:

O Heavenly King, the Comforter, the Spirit of Truth, who is in all places and fills all things, Treasury of blessings and giver of life: come and dwell in us, cleanse us from every stain, and save our souls, O gracious Lord.

PSALM

Awake to the Lord and his strength; seek his face always.

Awake, harp and lyre!
I will awaken the dawn.
(Psalm 108:2)

Awake to the Lord and his strength; seek his face always.

JESUS

Blessed are the merciful,
for they will be shown mercy. (from Matthew 5:3-9)

Lord Jesus Christ, Son of God, have mercy on me.

OPEN

A time for personal prayers.

After your own prayers, **Our Father,** then

In our lives and in our prayers, may your kingdom come.

SEAL

Blow out the candle? Put a stone in the water.?
Make the sign of the cross? Kneel and bow down?
Say the closing prayer.

May the peace of Christ go with us: wherever he may send us; wherever he may guide us; and bring us home rejoicing

MORNING

FOCUS

In the name of the Father, and the Son and the Holy Spirit.

Draw us into your love, Christ Jesus, and deliver us from fear.

Those who hope in the Lord will renew their strength.
They will soar on wings like eagles, they will run and not grow weary,
 they will walk and not be faint. (Isaiah 40:30-31).

Be still. Breath slowly. Give thanks.

TOUCH

We are more than our minds and our feelings. We are bodies. Respond and pray with
the body.

Light a candle?
Burn some incense?
Hold a prayer bead or stone?
Sprinkle some water over your face?
Stand or kneel?
Make the sign of the cross?
Hold out your open hands?

WELCOME

A prayer of introduction, welcome and praise:

**O Heavenly King, the Comforter, the Spirit of Truth, who is in all places and fills all
things, Treasury of blessings and giver of life: come and dwell in us, cleanse us
from every stain, and save our souls, O gracious Lord.**

PSALM

Great is God's faithfulness and love

Praise the Lord, all you nations, extol him, all you peoples,
for great is his love toward us and the faithfulness of the Lord endures forever.
(Psalm 117:1-2)

Great is God's faithfulness and love

JESUS

"The kingdom of God is within your midst." (Luke 17:21)

Lord Jesus Christ, Son of God, have mercy on me.

OPEN

A time for personal prayers.

After your own prayers, **Our Father,** then

In our lives and in our prayers, may your kingdom come.

SEAL

Blow out the candle? Put a stone in the water.?
Make the sign of the cross? Kneel and bow down?
Say the closing prayer.

May the peace of Christ go with us: wherever he may send us; wherever he may guide us; and bring us home rejoicing

ELEVENSES

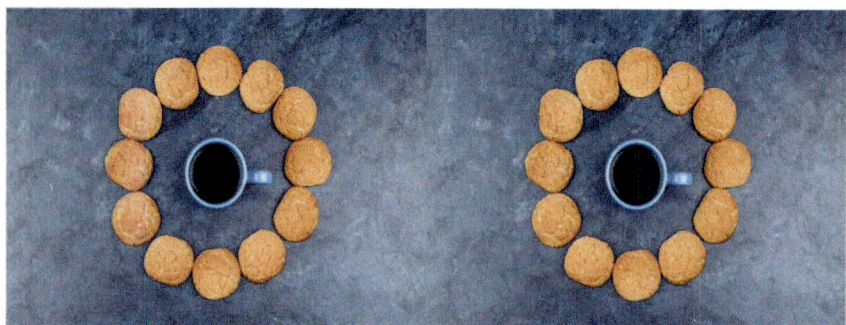

FOCUS

In the name of the Father, and the Son, and the Holy Spirit.

Draw us into your love, Christ Jesus, and deliver us from fear.

Those who hope in the Lord will renew their strength.
They will soar on wings like eagles, they will run and not grow weary,
 they will walk and not be faint. (Isaiah 40:30-31).

Be still. Breath slowly. Give thanks.

TOUCH

*We are more than our minds and our feelings. We are bodies. Respond and pray with the
body.*

Light a candle?
Burn some incense?
Hold a prayer bead or stone?
Sprinkle some water over your face?
Stand or kneel?
Make the sign of the cross?
Hold out your open hands?

WELCOME

A prayer of introduction, welcome and praise.

**O Heavenly King, the Comforter, the Spirit of Truth, who is in all places and fills all
things, Treasury of blessings and giver of life: come and dwell in us, cleanse us
from every stain, and save our souls, O gracious Lord.**

PSALM

You refresh my soul, Lord

You, God, are my God,
 earnestly I seek you;
I thirst for you,
 my whole being longs for you,
in a dry and parched land
 where there is no water.
(Psalm 63: 1)

You refresh my soul, Lord

JESUS

Peace, I leave with you; my peace I give you. I do not give to you as the world gives. Do not let your hearts be troubled and do not be afraid. (John 14:27)

Lord Jesus Christ, Son of God, have mercy on me.

OPEN

A time for personal prayers.

After your own prayers, **Our Father,** then

In our lives and in our prayers, may your kingdom come.

SEAL

Blow out the candle? Put a stone in the water.? Make the sign of the cross? Kneel and bow down?
Say the closing prayer,

May the peace of Christ go with us: wherever he may send us; wherever he may guide us; and bring us home rejoicing.

FOCUS

In the name of the Father, and the Son, and the Holy Spirit.

Draw us into your love, Christ Jesus, and deliver us from fear.

Those who hope in the Lord will renew their strength.
They will soar on wings like eagles, they will run and not grow weary,
 they will walk and not be faint. (Isaiah 40:30-31).

Be still. Breath slowly. Give thanks.

TOUCH

We are more than our minds and our feelings. We are bodies. Respond and pray with the body.

Light a candle?
Burn some incense?
Hold a prayer bead or stone?
Sprinkle some water over your face?
Stand or kneel?
Make the sign of the cross?
Hold out your open hands?

WELCOME

A prayer of introduction, welcome and praise.

O Heavenly King, the Comforter, the Spirit of Truth, who is in all places and fills all things, Treasury of blessings and giver of life: come and dwell in us, cleanse us from every stain, and save our souls, O gracious Lord.

PSALM

You are a shield around me, O Lord

But you, Lord, are a shield around me,
my glory, the One who lifts my head high.
I call out to the Lord,
and he answers me from his holy mountain.
(Psalm 5: 3-4)

You are a shield around me, O Lord

JESUS

Take my yoke upon you and learn from me, for I am gentle and humble in heart, and you
will find rest for your souls. (Matthew 11:29)

Lord Jesus Christ, Son of God, have mercy on me.

OPEN

A time for personal prayers.

After your own prayers, **Our Father,** then

In our lives and in our prayers, may your kingdom come.

SEAL

*Blow out the candle? Put a stone in the water.? Make the sign of the cross? Kneel and
bow down?*
Say the closing prayer,

**May the peace of Christ go with us: wherever he may send us; wherever he may
guide us; and bring us home rejoicing.**

AFTERNOON

FOCUS

In the name of the Father, and the Son, and the Holy Spirit.

Draw us into your love, Christ Jesus, and deliver us from fear.

Those who hope in the Lord will renew their strength.
They will soar on wings like eagles, they will run and not grow weary,
 they will walk and not be faint. (Isaiah 40:30-31).

Be still. Breath slowly. Give thanks.

TOUCH

We are more than our minds and our feelings. We are bodies. Respond and pray with the body.

Light a candle?
Burn some incense?
Hold a prayer bead or stone?
Sprinkle some water over your face?
Stand or kneel?
Make the sign of the cross?
Hold out your open hands?

WELCOME

A prayer of introduction, welcome and praise.

O Heavenly King, the Comforter, the Spirit of Truth, who is in all places and fills all things, Treasury of blessings and giver of life: come and dwell in us, cleanse us from every stain, and save our souls, O gracious Lord.

PSALM

I will rest in the shadow of the Almighty

Whoever dwells in the shelter of the Most High
 will rest in the shadow of the Almighty.
I will say of the Lord, "He is my refuge and my fortress,
my God, in whom I trust."
(Psalm 91:1-2)

I will rest in the shadow of the Almighty

JESUS

 My command is this: Love each other as I have loved you. Greater love has no one than this: to lay down one's life for one's friends. (John 15:12-13)

Lord Jesus Christ, Son of God, have mercy on me.

OPEN

A time for personal prayers.

After your own prayers, **Our Father,** then

In our lives and in our prayers, may your kingdom come.

SEAL

Blow out the candle? Put a stone in the water.? Make the sign of the cross? Kneel and bow down?
Say the closing prayer,

May the peace of Christ go with us: wherever he may send us; wherever he may guide us; and bring us home rejoicing.

EVENING

FOCUS

In the name of the Father, and the Son, and the Holy Spirit.

Draw us into your love, Christ Jesus, and deliver us from fear.

Those who hope in the Lord will renew their strength.
They will soar on wings like eagles, they will run and not grow weary,
they will walk and not be faint. (Isaiah 40:30-31).

Be still. Breath slowly. Give thanks.

TOUCH

We are more than our minds and our feelings. We are bodies. Respond and pray with the body.

Light a candle?
Burn some incense?
Hold a prayer bead or stone?
Sprinkle some water over your face?
Stand or kneel?
Make the sign of the cross?
Hold out your open hands?

WELCOME

A prayer of introduction, welcome and praise.

O Heavenly King, the Comforter, the Spirit of Truth, who is in all places and fills all things, Treasury of blessings and giver of life: come and dwell in us, cleanse us from every stain, and save our souls, O gracious Lord.

PSALM

I will call on him as long as I shall live

I love the Lord, for he heard my voice;
he heard my cry for mercy.
Because he turned his ear to me,
I will call on him as long as I live.
(Psalm 116:1-2)

I will call on him as long as I shall live

JESUS

Jesus answered, "Everyone who drinks this water will be thirsty again, [14] but whoever drinks the water I give them will never thirst. Indeed, the water I give them will become in them a spring of water welling up to eternal life." (John 14:13-14)

Lord Jesus Christ, Son of God, have mercy on me.

OPEN

A time for personal prayers.

After your own prayers, **Our Father,** then

In our lives and in our prayers, may your kingdom come.

SEAL

Blow out the candle? Put a stone in the water.? Make the sign of the cross? Kneel and bow down?
Say the closing prayer,

May the peace of Christ go with us: wherever he may send us; wherever he may guide us; and bring us home rejoicing.

NIGHT

FOCUS

In the name of the Father, the Son, and the Holy Spirit.

Draw us into your love, Christ Jesus, and deliver us from fear.

In peace I will lie down and sleep, for you alone, Lord,
make me dwell in safety. (Psalm 4:8)

Be still. Breath slowly. Think about your day. Be honest with yourself.

TOUCH

We are more than our minds and our feelings. We are bodies. Respond and pray with the body.

Light a candle?
Burn some incense?
Hold a prayer bead or stone?
Sprinkle some water over your face?
Stand or kneel?
Make the sign of the cross?
Hold out your open hands?

WELCOME

A prayer of introduction, welcome and praise.

O Heavenly King, the Comforter, the Spirit of Truth, who is in all places and fills all things, Treasury of blessings and giver of life: come and dwell in us, cleanse us from every stain, and save our souls, O gracious Lord.

PSALM

Great is God's faithfulness and love

Praise the Lord, all you nations, extol him, all you peoples,
for great is his love toward us and the faithfulness of the Lord endures forever.

Great is God's faithfulness and love

JESUS

Blessed are the peacemakers,
for they will be called children of God. (Matthew 5: 9)

Lord Jesus Christ, Son of God, have mercy on me.

OPEN

A time for personal prayers.

After your own prayers, **Our Father,** then

In our lives and in our prayers, may your kingdom come.

SEAL

Blow out the candle? Put a stone in the water.?
Make the sign of the cross? Kneel and bow down?
Say the closing prayer.

**May the peace of Christ go with us: wherever he may send us; wherever he may
guide us; and bring us home rejoicing**

MORE PSALMS AND JESUS?

There are seven alternative Psalms and sayings of Jesus below. The idea is that you can alternate the days with these if you wish.

PSALMS

DAWN

In the morning I will sing of your love

But I will sing of your strength, in the morning I will sing of your love; for you are my fortress, my refuge in times of trouble.
(Psalm 59:16)

In the morning I will sing of your love

MORNING

Love and faithfulness meet together

Love and faithfulness meet together;
righteousness and peace kiss each other.
Faithfulness springs forth from the earth,
and righteousness looks down from heaven.
The Lord will indeed give what is good,

and our land will yield its harvest.
Righteousness goes before him
and prepares the way for his steps.
(Psalm 85: 10-13)

Love and faithfulness meet together

ELEVENSES

For you are great and do marvellous deeds

Among the gods there is none like you, Lord;
no deeds can compare with yours.
All the nations you have made
will come and worship before you, Lord;
they will bring glory to your name.
 For you are great and do marvellous deeds;
you alone are God.
(Psalm 86: 8-10)

For you are great and do marvellous deeds

NOON

Your ways, God, are holy. What god is as great as our God?

I will remember the deeds of the Lord;
yes, I will remember your miracles of long ago.
 I will consider all your works
 and meditate on all your mighty deeds.
Your ways, God, are holy.
What god is as great as our God?
You are the God who performs miracles;
 you display your power among the peoples.
(Psalm 77: 11-14)

Your ways, God, are holy. What god is as great as our God?

AFTERNOON

With you, Lord, is unfailing love

One thing God has spoken,
two things I have heard:
"Power belongs to you, God,
and with you, Lord, is unfailing love";
and, "You reward everyone
according to what they have done."
(Psalm 62:11-12)

With you, Lord, is unfailing love

EVENING

May my prayer be set before you like incense

I call to you, Lord, come quickly to me;
hear me when I call to you.
May my prayer be set before you like incense;
may the lifting up of my hands be like the evening sacrifice.
(Psalm 141:1-2)

May my prayer be set before you like incense

NIGHT

Where can I go from your Spirit?

Where can I flee from your presence?
If I go up to the heavens, you are there;
if I make my bed in the depths, you are there.
If I rise on the wings of the dawn,
 if I settle on the far side of the sea,
even there your hand will guide me,
your right hand will hold me fast.
 If I say, "Surely the darkness will hide me
and the light become night around me,"
even the darkness will not be dark to you;
the night will shine like the day,
for darkness is as light to you.

(Psalm 139:7-12)
Where can I go from your Spirit?

JESUS

These sayings are some of the 'I am' sayings of Jesus that are found in the Gospel of John.

DAWN

Then Jesus declared, "I am the bread of life. Whoever comes to me will never go hungry, and whoever believes in me will never be thirsty." (John 6:35)

MORNING

When Jesus spoke again to the people, he said, "I am the light of the world. Whoever follows me will never walk in darkness but will have the light of life." (John 8:12)

ELEVENSES

"I am the gate; whoever enters through me will be saved. They will come in and go out and find pasture." (John 10:9)

NOON

"I am the good shepherd. The good shepherd lays down his life for the sheep." (John 10:11)

EVENING

Jesus said to her, "I am the resurrection and the life. The one who believes in me will live, even though they die." (John 11: 25)

NIGHT

Jesus answered, "I am the way and the truth and the life. No one comes to the Father except through me." (John 14:6)

LONGER?

Why not read the whole Psalm or Gospel passage that is quoted from?

Or, a bit more daring, start with Psalm 1 and then work gradually through them all per part of the day?

The same with the Gospels.

Perhaps, restrict this to MORNING and EVENING when there may be a little more time?

SONGS OF THE GOSPELS

BENEDICTUS

(The song of Zechariah)

Praise be to the Lord, the God of Israel,
  because he has come to his people and redeemed them.
He has raised up a horn[c] of salvation for us
  in the house of his servant David
as he said through his holy prophets of long ago),
salvation from our enemies
and from the hand of all who hate us—
to show mercy to our ancestors
and to remember his holy covenant,
the oath he swore to our father Abraham:
to rescue us from the hand of our enemies,
and to enable us to serve him without fear
in holiness and righteousness before him all our days.
And you, my child, will be called a prophet of the Most High;
for you will go on before the Lord to prepare the way for him,
to give his people the knowledge of salvation
through the forgiveness of their sins,
because of the tender mercy of our God,
by which the rising sun will come to us from heaven
to shine on those living in darkness
and in the shadow of death,
to guide our feet into the path of peace.

(Luke 1: 68-79)

MAGNIFICAT

Mary's Song

My soul glorifies the Lord
and my spirit rejoices in God my Savior,
for he has been mindful
of the humble state of his servant.
From now on all generations will call me blessed,
for the Mighty One has done great things for me—
holy is his name.
His mercy extends to those who fear him,
from generation to generation.
He has performed mighty deeds with his arm;
he has scattered those who are proud in their inmost thoughts.
He has brought down rulers from their thrones
but has lifted up the humble.
He has filled the hungry with good things
but has sent the rich away empty.
He has helped his servant Israel,
remembering to be merciful
to Abraham and his descendants forever,
just as he promised our ancestors.

(Luke 1: 46-55)

This is usually said/sung during Evening prayer.

NUNC DIMITTIS

Simeon's Song

Sovereign Lord, as you have promised,

you may now dismiss your servant in peace.

For my eyes have seen your salvation,

which you have prepared in the sight of all nations:

a light for revelation to the Gentiles,

and the glory of your people Israel.

(Luke 2: 29-32)

This is traditionally said/sung at Night Prayer

ROCK, PAPER, SCISSORS

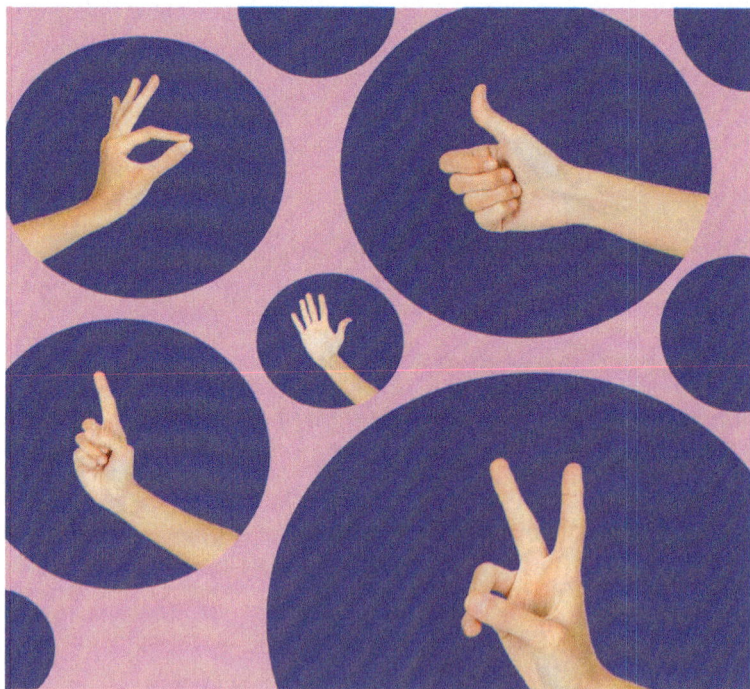

GET CREATIVE!
DO IT YOURSELF

There are seven empty circles in this section. Have a go at drawing or writing in one thing that sums up the time of day, such as maybe a rising sun for dawn, and so on.

What can you do with them?

Cut them out?

Stick on card?

Fix to the wall?

Glue into your diary?

Paste onto your desktop?

Make a necklace or bracelet using your designs painted on beads?

Or, seven different colours of beads?

Paint designs on pebbles, place in a bowl, or arrange on your desk?

Use one pebble with a word on it, or a symbol such as a cross?

Use your imagination. Play!

The idea is that when you look or touch any of these, you are in tune with the prayer time. Stop, be still, pray.

Besides these, use movements such as holding up your hands (even dance if you want to!).
Hold a small cross (especially the 'cross in the hand' that slips into your fingers).

Can you dance a prayer?

For some, dance expresses their hopes, their joy, their fears. Can you dance a prayer?
Of course, if this is your way, your gift.

USING INCENSE?

The use of incense in worship in very ancient. It was used in Jewish liturgy and not just pagan, as Psalm 141:2, "May my prayer be set before you like incense; may the lifting up of my hands be like the evening sacrifice" demonstrates.

Burning incense suggested prayers rising to God (or *before* God, if we do not wish to use the 'God up there' idea, as such). Furthermore, it could suggest being in the presence of something or someone special. It was scented, of a pleasant, perfumed aroma. Its small clouds suggested mystery, too, as worshippers stood in awe.

Incense was used in the Jerusalem Temple, and this practice was carried on by some Christians when praying, whether alone, or in the liturgy (particularly at the eucharist – the holy communion).

If you want to use incense at home, then you can buy small holders, pieces of special charcoal and incense grains, or just use joss sticks.

Holy Pictures

I remember visiting a bereaved woman when I was in Anglican ministry. She reached out for a photo of her beloved husband and traced her finger lovingly over it. As a tear touched her cheek, I reflected how this was akin to the use of holy images for some people. Writing about statues and paintings might not be something you are easy with. Aren't they 'graven images' (cf Exodus 20:3-5)? Aren't these forbidden? What was forbidden was worshipping any statues or pictures (of anything), and any superstition and magic that might be attached to them. This was a common pagan practice, after all.

In Christian tradition, nonetheless, there are many statues and paintings of Jesus, Mary and the Saints. Why? They are not to be worshipped. They are like visual aids, akin to the bereaved woman I mentioned earlier. The photo of the deceased was not actually her husband, and it could not bring him back, and she honoured and loved it it did not worship it. Holy images are such visual aids that can be moving. They can nudge and encourage people to pray.

For some, 2D images will be more congenial than 3D ones. Others do not wish to use such things at all. If they are used in prayer, how so? You can simply look at the picture and what it suggests. You might touch it, or even kiss it in reverence. Eastern Orthodox Christians have very ancient and particular rules for making holy images, called 'icons'. These show Christ, Mary and the Saints in a set fashion. There are often many little symbols contained in the illustrations, too. They use golden hues for part of the design suggesting holiness. Those of Mary, it should be noted, often have her holding the Christ child and pointing a finger towards him, or she stands, hands raised in prayer and worship, with a Christ child in her womb reaching his arms out in welcome and blessing.

So, use them if it helps. Do try to understand what they are and what they are not meant to be. If you can't cope with this type of devotional prayer, then find what is helpful and inspiring for you, no worries.

Praying with Holy Pictures

Orthodox Christians refer to icons as

'Windows into Heaven'.

CREATE

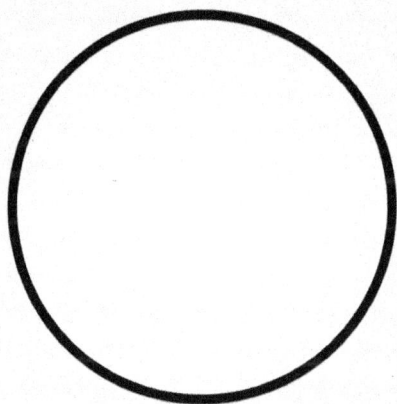

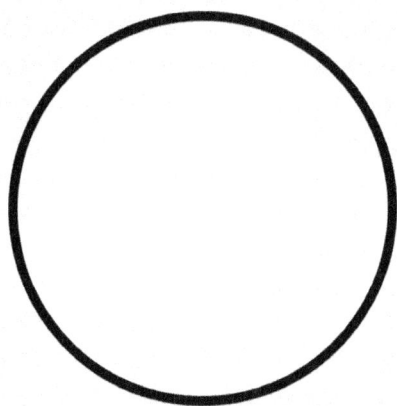

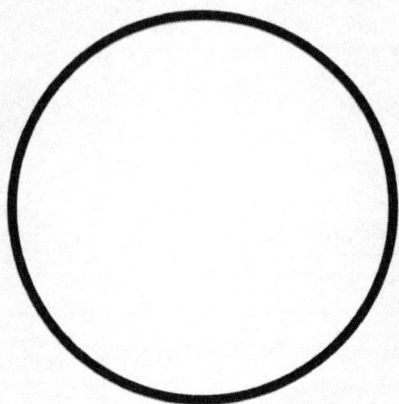
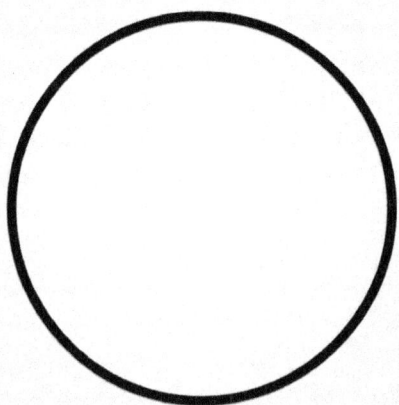

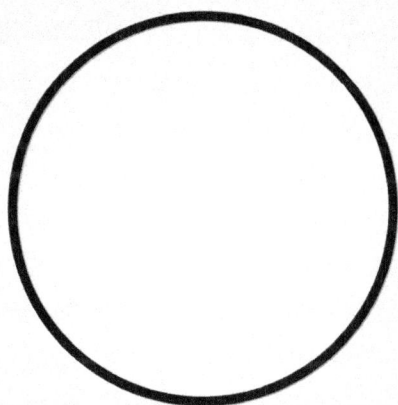

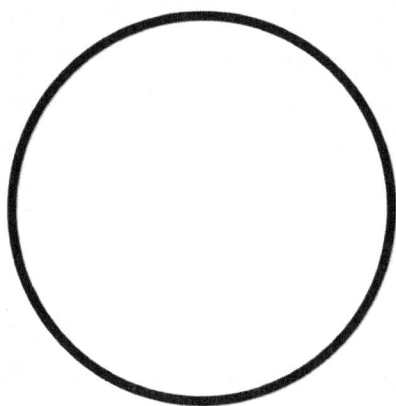

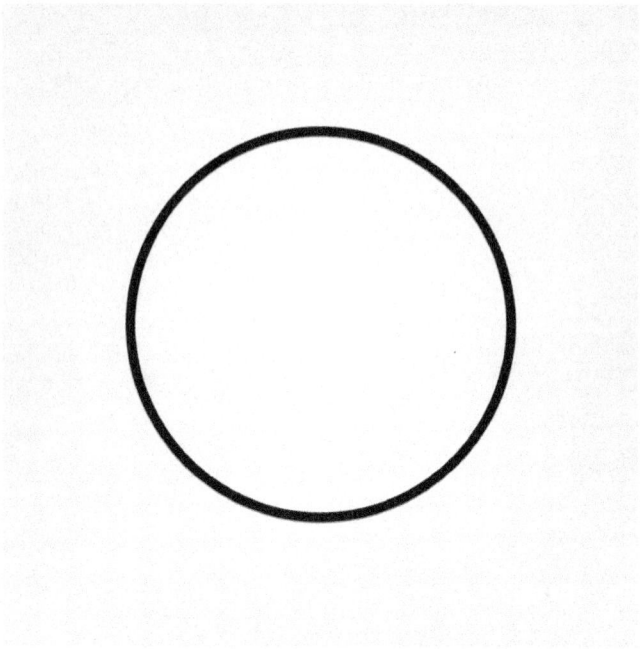

Draw, paint, colour, write, your own designs in each circle for Dawn, Morning, Elevenses, Noon, Afternoon, Evening and Night.